In Praise of 40 Day Tone of Voice Tone Down

*I was so excited when the **Tone of Voice Tone Down** was created. Charlotte Avery has a gentle, yet matter of fact, way of sharing God's heart for us to speak to others in and with love. The **Tone of Voice Tone Down** has helped me communicate better with my son. And on those days I don't get it right, I can hear Charlotte's words say, "Yesterday is gone...But TODAY you have been gifted another day to get 'it' RIGHT" (4.11.16 TVTD FB post). Thank you for speaking life.*

*- Aurellia Anderson, Author, **Lipgloss, Blazers, & Shoes: Knowing Your Identity and Purpose** (2015)*

*As parents of three active boys, this book is a God-send! In just a few weeks of applying the principles outlined in **Tone of Voice Tone Down** my husband and I have revolutionized how we interact with our sons. What's even better is that Charlotte isn't just sharing ideas she's heard, as a mom of seven she's sharing what she **knows**. I highly recommend this book if you're looking to create a more peaceful home environment.*

- Rev. Ronné Wingate Sims

40 Day Tone of Voice Tone Down

**Transform Your Relationships
One Octave at a Time**

Charlotte E. Avery

40 Day Tone of Voice Tone Down
"Transform Your Relationships One Octave at a Time"
By,
Charlotte E. Avery
© 2015 Being Charlotte Avery, Mythikos Mommy, LLC & Charlotte E. Avery

ISBN: 978-0-9819941-1-6
LCCN: 2016908275

Dedication

My Husband & Children

*I dedicate this book to my husband, the Head Coach of my
family and to our seven children, The A-Team.*

*There is nothing I can say that could ever express
how much I love all of you. You have been the
recipients of words that have harmed and words that have
healed which have come directly from my mouth
AND YET, you love me unconditionally.
You are the reasons that I strive to be a better
me every single day of my life.*

I love you today, tomorrow, and always.

To My Mom,
I love You

To the Readers,
I understand.

Contents

Foreword

When it comes to taming the tongue, Charlotte Avery has some advice for all of us. According to Charlotte, what we say is just as important as how we say it. Tone of voice can make or break friendships, can destroy personal and professional relationships, and can cause irreparable damage to family bonds. You can hear tone over the phone. You can even detect tone in a text, email, or social media post. What often could be mended by having a simple face-to-face meeting or discussion can be misconstrued by a few well-placed capitalized words, exclamation points, or Emojis!

While reading this power-packed resource, reflect on your own behavior. We are often quick to call others out on their bad behaviors, yet refuse to check ourselves. In *Tone of Voice Tone Down*, the journey of self-discovery may anger you, may annoy you, and may even cause you to laugh at yourself.

Charlotte Avery's 40 Day *Tone of Voice Tone Down* challenges you to be a better person from the inside out. Take time for yourself each day for the next 40 days to discover what your life can be with a new *tone of voice*.

Jacquie Hood Martin, Ph.D

What They Are Saying

Explosive, reactive, and loud. All words used to describe my response in stressful situations before partaking of *Tone of Voice Tone Down*. This book has equipped me with helpful tools that remind me to think, pause, and pray before I respond. "No matter how hard it gets... KEEP IT MOVING!!!"

– Zalika S. Brown

The 40-Day *Tone of Voice Tone Down* helped me in more ways than you could imagine. I've always seemed to be that mom that could go from 0 to 1000 in 2 seconds flat, especially being a single parent always seeming to feel overwhelmed, acting as though there was not enough time in a day to complete all my tasks or have time to myself. Every little thing seemed to frustrate me, but the things that frustrated me the most were the cat fights and nit picking between my kids. I would always seem to deal with the situation by yelling, fussing, and even at times hollering at the top of my lungs, not realizing this was only making matters worse and leaving my children with the impression that they were simply a bother to me more than anything else. When I started this 40-day challenge, I knew I had to do something to change. The first week was hard. But when I realized I had to do what was best for me and for my children, it seemed to change a lot of how I responded to various situations. I even began to see a change in my children. I'm not saying I don't have my moments where I reach 1000, but they are just few and far between. I enjoyed the *Tone of Voice Tone Down* challenge because it allowed me to see some things about myself that

I did not want my children to mirror in their future. Thank you for allowing me to be a part of such a positive and impactful group.

– Nicole Roberts

Being a part of the ***Tone of Voice Tone Down*** Facebook group made me more aware of my tone to not only my husband, but family, friends, and even at times co-workers. The Biblical references and testimonies of others challenged me to do better and ensured me that I was not on this journey alone. Now, I would love to say that I have mastered it totally without any slip-ups but that would not be the truth. However, I will say I am better with managing my mouth than when the group started. And though I don't get it right every time, I believe whole heartedly…that the God who started this great work in me will keep at it and bring it to a flourishing finish on the very day Christ Jesus appears (Phil 1:6, MSG).

Thank you Charlotte for being obedient to the voice of the Lord. My husband and future children thank you also.

– Rasheda Persinger

So thankful for the ***Tone of Voice Tone Down*** which revealed how my raised voice, disposition, and sarcasm affected the people closest to me – my children. As a single parent, it is easy to feel alone in the battle, to question whether you are making the right decisions, and to stress over how every action will affect your child's self-esteem and ultimately, his or her future.

My youngest daughter has ADHD. Regardless of what some may say, ADHD is real. She has real struggles every day with attention issues, impulsiveness, and social skills. The things most children take for granted are so difficult for her, like developing lasting friendships. As a parent, I know that I am the greatest influence on her self-esteem. That is why ***Tone of Voice Tone Down*** was so important to me. I am learning to speak words that will encourage and build her up instead of tearing her down by accepting my imperfections and allowing my children to see those imperfections by knowing when to apologize (a tough one), and by disciplining with love. I am still a work in progress!

Tone of Voice Tone Down is a constant reminder of what I strive for. I am grateful for my sister Charlotte for her obedience to God. I expect to see the fruit of this labor for years to come!

– Lisa T.

Introduction

Are you tone of voice challenged? Are you tired of breaking the hearts of your children, spouse, family, friends, co-workers, or others because you sometimes, usually, or often yell or raise your voice? Do you have the tendency to be hurtful through sarcastic, condescending, or patronizing words and tones? If so, then this book is for you. Do you know someone who is challenged in this area? If so, this book is for them.

I have heard many leaders and motivators say that anything you can do for 21 days or longer becomes a habit. The *40 Day Tone of Voice Tone Down Transformation* will challenge you to conquer your habit of raising your voice, yelling, and using inappropriate tones, and to create a new habit of speaking with the appropriate tone of voice.

This book is here to empower you to do better and to be a better person to yourself, your spouse, your children, your coworkers, and others. Along with this book, you will be able to join a community where you can find strength, encouragement, and support. You will be able to appropriately vent, ask questions, and give praise reports without judgment.

How will we do this?

- For the next 40 days you will have a scripture and quick thought every morning to meditate on throughout the day.

- You will not be allowed to yell, raise your voice, or use sarcastic and patronizing tones to communicate with anyone in or outside of your home.
- You will not be allowed to yell throughout your house to get the attention of anyone unless it is a major emergency. If you want the attention of someone that is not near you, you must make an effort to go where they are or wait for them to come to you.
- You will need to find at least one person to tell about your issue and why you are doing this transformation.
- You will have a Daily Progress Page. On that page you will journal your progress each day.

I know old habits die hard, but there is too much at stake if we don't have self-control and control our tone of voice. If you slip up, DO NOT get frustrated and DO NOT quit. Apologize to the one(s) you offended, repent, ask for forgiveness, STAY THE COURSE, and KEEP MOVING FORWARD!!!

The fact that you have decided to go on this 40 Day journey with me is a major first step. I commend you for your truth and your honesty. I am excited about being on this journey with you. May God bless and reward all of us as we strive to conquer this area of our lives. May we and those connected to us be blessed by the transformation that is coming.

(((HUGS))),

Charlotte

1

The Post that Started It All

The Post that Started It All

Below is the first post I ever blogged about my tone of voice.

Old Yeller

September 4, 2010

Almost 12 weeks ago I was sitting in the hair salon under the dryer when I came across a blog post by Veronica Webb. Her post entitled "A Quiet House" hit me in the face like a ton of bricks. I think I still have the marks on my face. Anyway, in her article she was talking about how she used to yell at her children as a form of discipline and out of frustration. She got to the point where she decided that yelling at her children was not what she wanted. One of her children asked her why she yelled. She shared things with them about her childhood and so on. She apologized to her children and told them that from that day forward she would not yell at them, with the exception of dangerous and urgent situations.

Now, let me just say, I naturally have a loud and very strong voice. I am not one who needs a microphone to talk to a group of people. To be quite honest, I have been a yeller for quite some time. If you don't believe me, ask my older brother. However, I thank Veronica Webb for her blog post because what she was talking about really hit home for me. Just a week before I read her blog post, I committed in my heart that I would stop yelling at my children. I was just a month or so out from having my fifth baby when I realized that my tone of voice was getting out of control. Granted, I was beyond exhausted and often times frustrated that a few things weren't going my way, but that was no reason to yell at my husband or my children. The thing that did it for me was when I yelled at my daughter about something. My voice was so out of control that she had a look of fear in her eyes and tears ran down her face as her little voice said, "Mommy, Mommy, I didn't mean it." When I reached for her she jumped. The look of fear in her eyes hurt me to my core. And the fact that she jumped when I reached for her hurt me also. In another instance, I was so beyond frustrated with my husband one day that I yelled at him in front of the children. I was so mad that the tone and volume of my voice was so out of control that my son came by the door and said, "Mommy, you are supposed to be kind to Daddy. You are not being kind one to another." What on earth was I thinking? With all the things that my children are confronted with in the world outside our home, the last person who they need to feel abused, violated, or afraid of is me, their mommy, the one who pushed them into this world. From that point on, I knew that I NEEDED to do better. I HAD to do better. I WANTED to do better. If I don't do better, I will be damaging the lives of the people who need and love me most.

In closing, there are a few things that I really appreciated about the blog post by Veronica Webb.

1. This celebrity was not afraid to expose her flaws to the public and to her children.

2. She was big enough to apologize and explain her behavior to her children.

3. She recognized that having A Quiet Home started with her.

4. She understood the power that she had as the mother of her children.

5. One of the last things that she said is that she doesn't strive to be a perfect mother; she strives to be a better mother.

Today, I want to confess that I love being a mommy. I confess that motherhood is a HARD job. I confess that everything does not run smoothly in my home every single day. I also confess that my name is Charlotte and I am a recovering yeller. I am proud to say that I am almost 12 weeks sober from yelling.

Here is to all the mommies who strive to be better because they understand that perfection is out of reach.

Stay Fabulous!!!

2

I Fell off the Wagon Again… and Again

I Fell off the Wagon Again... and Again

Iwould like to say that after posting that blog post that I got it together and never yelled at my husband or children again. However, that would be so very far from the truth. To be honest, I fell off the wagon again and again. Every time I fell off the wagon I was stricken with grief and shame. Yes, I apologized. Yes, I said, "I love you." Yes, I said I would never do it again. But I did do it again, more times than I can count and more times than I want to remember. I fell off the wagon so many times that even today I pray that God will wipe it from the minds and hearts of my loved ones.

One day after having a major yelling fit, I came to a place where I needed to do some major soul searching. I was having a lack of self-control. I was tired of always having to apologize for the same old thing. I was tired of having days or weeks of success only to relapse into my old behavior. I was tired of getting on and off the wagon.

If I was going to stop my behavior, I was going to have to do some hard work and ask myself some hard questions that would get to the root or my deplorable deeds. I was going to have to get to the root of my behavior. I mean, something has to be majorly wrong with a woman who has an amazing husband, incredible children, and yells all of the time. Something had to be wrong with a person that was loving and gentle one minute but was damaging the next minute. I knew that my habitual actions were horrible, but I just couldn't get them under control. Something was wrong.

The first question I asked myself was:

Why was I yelling?

To be painfully and shamefully transparent, I was yelling because it made me feel powerful. It made me feel like I had control. It was something that I could do to control others and get my way. Because I could not control situations, people or circumstances in my childhood, I was determined to control them in my adulthood to the detriment of my husband and children.

Like most women, I got married wanting to be a loving, submissive, caring, and nurturing wife. I got married wanting to love, honor, and obey my husband through sickness and in health. I really did. I mean, God had blessed me with a gentle yet sometimes stubborn giant. He is handsome, humorous, hardworking, compassionate, giving, loving, God fearing, and he can reach the top shelf in the cabinets without a stepstool. YET, there was a part of me, the Eve part, that bucked up against it. And it didn't help that I was still dealing with unresolved daddy issues.

While my husband married me for all my "absolutely amazing" qualities, he also married me knowing the hurts in my life. He married me knowing that I am spirited (strong-willed), have great leadership skills (bossy), am sometimes stubborn, and struggle with money management. He knew that I had been through quite a bit. Yet he still chose me to be his wife, and for that I am forever thankful. And though he is not perfect, he is perfect for me.

We weren't too long into our marriage when he saw the not so pretty side of me. To this day, I don't remember what we were disagreeing about. All I remember was being so mad that I stormed out of our living room and went into our bathroom. He was determined to make his point, and I was determined not to hear or be anywhere near him. As I stormed off, he was hot on my trail. When I got to the bathroom,

I slammed the door. The mirror that was on the back of the door fell off and almost hit him. The mirror did not break. However, had that mirror hit him, it would have cut him, and I would have never forgiven myself. His mother would have never forgiven me, either. Even now, I am ashamed of that incident. And while I would like to say that was the only time that I yelled or slammed a door, it wasn't. Yet he has helped and loved me though it all.

You already know my story about Old Yeller. You would have thought that after coming into a revelation of myself and my behavior and writing that blog post that I would have stopped yelling and acting out, but I didn't. I had done a lot more damage with my words and behavior before I had a pivotal "come to Jesus" moment.

Just as I have been transparent and told you why I was yelling, you need to ask yourself the same question.

Why am I yelling?

_____

_____

_____

_____

_____

_____

_____

_____

Where or who did I get this behavior from?

My parents divorced when I was eight years old. While their marriage had some sore spots, there was no time that I ever remember either of them yelling. However, there were times when I felt there should have been some yelling.

Even now I can remember a time when my dad had done something that hurt my mom. To this day, I don't know what he did. But what I do know is that whatever he did, it crushed her spirit. I know this because while blow drying and pressing my hair she quietly wept.

When I asked her what was wrong, she said everything would be okay. I knew everything was not going to be okay and I was mad that my sweet, loving mom was hurt. I was mad and I wanted to do something about it. I wanted to protect her, but I was just a kid; and what was a seven-year-old going to do?

That was only one of many occasions when I felt hopeless and unable to express my hurt that later turned into rage that I carried from childhood into my adult years.

While my mom is a very gentle, meek, giving, gracious and forgiving woman, her mother was not. For an equivalent of a year and a half, my brother and I lived with my grandparents. My grandpa was a gentle giant. He was loving, kind, humble, humorous, compassionate, and God fearing. My grandmother, on the other hand, was very physically, emotionally, and verbally abusive. She had the appearance of being God fearing, but her behavior showed something completely different. Yes, she was a yeller. At the drop of a dime she could haul off and hit, yell, or curse at you for almost no reason.

I remember a time when she was doing my hair. I had very thick hair. On this particular occasion while she was doing my hair, I accidentally dropped a comb and a tooth broke out of it. Before I could apologize she picked up the comb, hit me in the head, yelled, and called me stupid.

Another time when I was in the fourth grade, I was sitting at her kitchen table reading out loud. I was not the best reader. While I was reading to her, I stumbled over words and read very slowly. Again, she ridiculed me, yelled at me, and called me stupid.

On another occasion, I remember my grandma had a doctor's appointment. My grandpa ended up working late and forgot to pick us up. By the time he arrived, she was furious. She was so furious that she hit him, yelled, and then got out of the car to walk home. Even after her belligerent behavior, he begged her to get back in the car. I don't know how far she walked, but at some point her feet must have been hurting in the high heels she was wearing because she got back in the car. When we got home it was not a good situation at all.

While there were moments of peace in my grandparents' home, those moments never seemed to last very long. We always walked on eggshells not knowing when her next fit of anger was going to come. Needless to say, I never looked forward to being at my grandparents' house. And I promised myself two things:

1. I will never be like my grandmother

2. If my grandmother was living when I had children, my children would not be around her.

Yet somewhere along the way, I started to display the behavior of the woman that I never wanted to be like. It is hard to believe that a year and a half of my life influenced me so much, but it did. And I hated it! So there you have it. I got my yelling behavior from my grandmother. Now, I want you to ask yourself the same question:

Where or who did I get this behavior from?

_____

_____

_____

_____

_____

_____

_____

What triggered me to yell?

One thing that I know about being a yeller is that there is always something that triggers the behavior. *The Merriam Webster Learner Dictionary* define a trigger as something that causes something to happen.

If I was going to overcome being a yeller, I really have to find out what caused me to be out of control to the point that I would yell.

After doing a self-inventory, I was able to nail down what my triggers were. Here are the top five things that triggered my very inappropriate behavior:

- Tiredness
- Feelings of inadequacy
- Feeling like I had no control
- Feelings from childhood hurt
- Trust issues

Tiredness

I know it's hard to believe, but yes, I get tired. I am a very busy wife and mom of seven high energy children. On my down time, I make breakfast, lunch and dinner. I am an errand runner, chauffer, and maid. I am a baby whisperer and potty training expert. I am a coach, manager, and personal shopper. I am an organizer, interior decorator, and laundry service. I am an uncertified nurse/physician's assistant who cleans and mends boo boos, while wiping tears. I also hold group counselling services three, maybe five times a week, specializing in team building exercises. I am also a storyteller, homework checker, and family photographer. I am always prepared to give hugs and Eskimo and fish-lip kisses. In between those duties, I run two companies, try to make time to stay in shape, and make sure I have enough time to invest in my marriage.

Do I do a lot? Yes. Am I under paid? Yes. Is my work rewarding? Yes. Am I exhausted at the end of the day? Yes. Does any of that justify my yelling, screaming, slamming doors, belittling, hurting, or breaking the hearts and spirit of my loved ones? NO!!!

Because I am constantly on the go from sun up to sun down, and sometimes in my sleep, I had to find ways to take care of myself. Self-care is a word that we hear often but we are horrible at practicing. I realized that taking care of everything and everybody else was making me tired, frustrated, and sometimes hostile. I also realized that I, along with you, am responsible for my own self-care. My joy, health, peace, and wholeness is my responsibility and no one else's. There is no way you can function optimally as a spouse, parent, caregiver, employer, etc. if you are not properly taking care of yourself. Choosing to take care of yourself first is not being selfish. Choosing to take care of yourself allows you to have the willingness and the capacity to take care of someone else.

You can practice self- care by doing some of the following:

- Getting proper rest
- Going for a walk
- Going to a movie
- Spending time with friends
- Taking a trip
- Going on a personal retreat
- Listening to music
- Going shopping
- Going to the gym
- Taking an uninterrupted bath or shower
- Journaling
- Taking a drive (not to pick up your children)
- Having lunch by yourself
- Going to a spa (not the grocery store)

These are just a few things you can do for self-care. Because my life is so busy, my goal is to do at least one thing a week that is just for me and no one else. I don't feel bad about it. And although my husband and children "may" miss me while I'm gone, they know that I will come back a better me.

Feelings of inadequacy

It is hard for some people to believe that I struggle with feelings of inadequacy. To say that I have come a long way, Baby, is an understatement. However, even at 40 something years old, I sometimes question whether or not I am good enough.

Although I am an author, speaker, Family System Strategist ™, have two degrees, and other accomplishments, I sometimes deal with the pain of being talked about for being held back a grade, wearing glasses, and not being a good reader in elementary school. I sometimes wonder if I am the right shade of brown because "being light was right". And there is never a time when I am about to speak to a group of people that I don't have to deal with wondering if I am going to look or sound "stupid."

From elementary school to grad school, I was always petrified to read out loud. When I became a mom, I was petrified even more. I knew that at some point I would have to read stories to my children and I did not want to stutter or sound "stupid" reading to them.

I know that feelings of inadequacy are very real. I know how they can make you feel insecure, give you feelings of jealousy and anxiety, cause you to lash out, even at those who love you. I also know that if not dealt with, feelings of inadequacy will steal meaningful relationships from you. They will prevent you from walking in your purpose. If not dealt with, those feelings will paralyze you from taking steps that will propel you to your God ordained destiny and purpose.

If you are struggling with feelings of inadequacy, then today is the day for you to be free. You can be by:

- Recognizing what they are
- Confronting where they came from
- Realizing they are a lie and not your reality
- Conquering them with boldness and truth

Feeling like I had no control

When I was younger, there were things in my life that I had no control of. I had no control over my parents getting divorced. I had no control over having to live with my grandparents. I had no control over some of the things I had been exposed to. I had no control over being held back in elementary school. I had no control over decisions and choices that people made that affected me. And the list goes on and on. Because there were so many things I could not control as a child and adolescent, I decided that my adult years would be different.

Feeling like I had no control in my youth produced fertile ground for me to be a "great leader" (controller) as an adult. Once I became an adult and no longer lived in my mom's house, I was determined to control everything and everybody that I could. While that might have been good for the workplace, it was certainly not good for my home life. Especially when I am also married to a controller.

When my husband and I got married I was still working. And whenever we would have a disagreement and my tone got loud he would say, "Charlotte, YOU ARE NOT GOING TO TALK ME LIKE THAT." And while he was saying it, I would sometimes roll my eyes and say, "Roderick, YOU ARE NOT THE BOSS OF ME!" Then he would say, "You may talk to so and so like that BUT YOU ARE NOT GOING TO TALK TO ME LIKE THAT."

You would think that after a few years of marriage, and a thousand apologies, that I would have stopped yelling at my husband, but I didn't. It was not until Proverbs 21:9 was brought to my attention that I got a clear picture of the damage that I was doing to my marriage. That passage reads, "It's better to live alone in the corner of an attic than with a quarrelsome wife in a lovely home". (NLT).

When I read that passage I felt like I had gotten hit in my face with a huge brick. I actually felt sick to my stomach. That passage was everything that I did not want to do or be to my husband. That passage was a reflection of what I was doing all the while being like the person that I did not want to be. I read that passage over and over again and I sobbed. In my mind, all I could see was having moments of no self-control, yelling, and being belligerent to the gift that God had given me in the form of my husband. It did not matter that I kept our house clean, prepared his meals, or anything else. What mattered was that I was being hurtful, disrespectful, and out of control because I wanted control.

All I could see was the man that I loved and who loved me, sitting out on top of our roof feeling unloved and exposed to the elements. Not only was he being exposed to the elements, but he was noticing and being noticed by others. And while he was being exposed, so was I. God used that verse to shake me to my core. He used it to show me that if I kept going down this dark road, my marriage could suffer in a horrible way that would have been caused by my own words and my own behavior. Did being in control matter more to me than my marriage did? Absolutely not. I had to make a change.

What I just shared with you is my truth and I'm sticking to it. I am not proud of it but it is my truth. I am proud to say that I am better today than I was yesterday. But let me ask you, "What is your truth?" Do you have control issues? If so, what are they and why do you have them? Are you willing to sacrifice your marriage or other relationships because of control issues or the lack thereof? I hope your answer is, NO. I hope that you are motivated to do the 40 Day Tone of Voice Tone Down and do what it takes to be a better you for yourself, your spouse, your children, and loved ones.

Feelings from childhood hurt

One thing I know for sure is that people who don't deal with their childhood hurt, pain, and suffering, turn out to be adults who intentionally or unintentionally cause hurt, pain, and suffering to others. I know that to be true because I have been the giver and recipient of such behavior. Any psychologist or counselor will tell you that hurting children usually turn out to be hurting adults.

There are many things that I wish I had not had to deal with during my youth and adolescent years. I can't change what happened; I can't change who hurt me. I don't have the power to resurrect anyone from the dead and make them apologize to me. The only person I can change is me. That is why the prayer of serenity is so important. Most people only know the first part of that prayer. This is how the entire prayer reads:

Serenity Prayer

Reinhold Niebuhr (1892-1971)

***God grant me the serenity
to accept the things I cannot change;
courage to change the things I can;***

and wisdom to know the difference.

Living one day at a time;
enjoying one moment at a time;
accepting hardships as the pathway to peace;
taking, as He did, this sinful world
as it is, not as I would have it;
trusting that He will make all things right
if I surrender to His Will;
that I may be reasonably happy in this life
and supremely happy with Him
forever in the next.
Amen.

http://www.beliefnet.com/Prayers/Protestant/Addiction/Serenity-Prayer.
aspx#6VqZPwHm8hfGGMsW.99

That prayer is not just good for those who are suffering with drug and alcohol addiction. It is good for people just like me and you.

One thing that you need to know is that no matter what someone has done or said that hurt you, you ALWAYS have a choice of what you say, how you say it, and how you treat other people. Yelling is a choice. The golden rule says that we are to treat others the way we want to be treated. Are you doing that with your words and behavior?

Trust issues

Yes, in my 40 something years of life, I have been through a lot. And because I had been through a lot, I had a lot of trust issues. I had trust issues with men and women. Those trust issues invaded my marriage. Some of my trust issues were valid, but the majority of them were not valid at all.

The more I think about it, the more I know that I was supposed to marry my husband. I mean, who on earth in their right mind would put up with all of my craziness, my loud mouth, and moments of blatant disrespect? Jeepers!!!

One time my husband came home late from work. I was beyond frustrated for several reasons:

1. He did not call to say that he was coming home late.

2. He did not answer his phone at work or cellphone when I called. (I called at least a gazillion times)

3. Dinner that I made got cold.

4. I was worried as a jitter bug.

5. This was not the first time that he didn't call and he knew how I felt about it.

When he got home, I looked at him to see if he was okay. Once I saw that he was, I blasted him. I was furious in a way that he had never seen. I said some things, and at the time, I meant every word that I said. It took me hours to get myself together. Sidebar, you should know that from the time we got married, we had rules of engagement when it came to being mad. The main rule was that we could not go to bed mad. On this night, we did not go to bed for a long time. And when I tried to go to sleep, he yanked the covers off of me and said, "I know you are not trying to go to sleep. WAKE UP!!!"

When I finally came to myself and was at a place where I could talk like a rational person, I realized that what made me explode was the fact that I had trust issues that stemmed way back to when my parents were married. I couldn't process it all at the time; but, nonetheless, he apologized, I apologized, and we went to bed.

A few years down the road he did something else, and I flew off the handle. I was so mad because I promised myself that I was not ever going to yell again, but I did.

After a while I began to see a pattern. The pattern that I began to see was all too familiar. Finally, I had an ah-ha moment. I realized that I was yelling at my husband because of trust issues that were a result of abandonment issues. The pain of my abandonment issues were oozing into my marriage. I was going to a place of ugly that I was afraid of and did not like. The abandonment issues that I dealt with from the first man in my life were creeping into my marriage. Not only was I not trusting, I was hostile, angry, and controlling. I was determined to take control and not relive my childhood. Yet I was reliving it and I hated it.

After I discovered the root of my foolishness, I shared it with my husband. He was so loving and understanding. He even apologized for doing certain things that triggered my feelings. Following his apology, he looked at me and said six words that shifted our marriage. He said, "Charlotte, I am not your dad."

His saying those words and the way he said them touched a place in me that I didn't even know existed. They spoke life into me and resurrected a place that had died. He said those words at the right place and right time. And I am forever grateful. It was at that moment when I felt relieved and compelled to be the wife that I was meant to be and the wife he was meant to have.

For me it was trust issues; for you it may be something else. I encourage you to find out what it is that is preventing you from having happy, healthy, and whole relationships with the people in your life? Ask yourself:

What are the triggers that cause me to yell?

_____

_____

_____

_____

After I identified my triggers, the things that caused me to yell and be out of control, I had to deal with how my words and actions affected and infected my loved ones. It was not good enough for me to know that I had scarred my husband and children. I had to go to them and ask how my bad behavior made them feel.

How did it make my loved ones feel?

While yelling made me feel powerful and in control, it made my loved ones feel hurt, disrespected, unloved, afraid, and anxious. It made them feel unappreciated, devalued, invalidated, and manipulated.

Even now, it pains me to know that I caused those feelings. Those are not feelings that anyone should feel from the people they love. Although I know I am forgiven, I feel like I will be spending the rest of my life making up for the damage that I have caused with my mouth.

While I used to be quick to speak before I think, today I am quick to think before I speak. And every time I get the notion to get mad and say something I regret, I am swift to remember the tube of toothpaste that I was given on my wedding day.

On the day that I got married, my matron of honor gave me a tube of toothpaste. When she gave it to me she said, "Charlotte, this is a tube of toothpaste. I want you to always remember that your words are just like the toothpaste in this tube. Just like you can't put toothpaste back in a tube, you can't take your words back once you have said them." Can you believe it? Even on my wedding day, God knew I was going to have problems with my mouth after I said, "I Do."

Today, I am very conscientious about my words and how they make people feel. What about you? Ask yourself the same question:

How does it make my loved ones feel when I yell?

_____

_____

_____

_____

_____

_____

_____

_____

How did it make me feel when I was yelling?

As I previously stated, yelling made me feel powerful and in control. However, moments after I yelled or had some fit of rage, I felt horrible and out of control. I felt naked and exposed. I felt embarrassed and ashamed. I felt like my husband was going to leave and my children would hate me. I felt like a liar, a terrorist, a fraud, and a bully. I felt unloving and mean. I felt remorseful and condemned. I felt miserable and downright low. I was becoming what I most feared. I was becoming a verbal abuser, a monster, and a tyrant. I was a verbal predator. You may not want to read those words, but it is my truth. Do you see yourself in any of those words? If so, then you are reading the right book at the right time. If you want to conquer this area of your life you have to confront yourself and ask:

How do I feel when I am yelling?

_____

_____

_____

_____

_____

_____

_____

_____

What was I getting out of yelling?

One thing I know for sure is that people who continue to yell or repeatedly engage in negative behavior do so for a few reasons:

1. There is a payoff or benefit to their negative behavior.
2. There hasn't been a severe enough consequence to make them stop.
3. They have not been confronted about their behavior.
4. They just don't care.

The first three reasons were certainly true as it pertained to me. The payoff that I got from yelling was that I felt strong, powerful and in control. It allowed me to manipulate others to get what I want. But the truth was that yelling masked my weaknesses, and it also exposed them. And while I felt strong and powerful, I was very much out of control.

Although my husband had confronted me several times about my behavior, others didn't. My children certainly didn't confront me because they were afraid of what I would do or say. When they spoke to me about my behavior they did so by way of their dad. He was their mediator. Every time he told me what they said, I would justify my actions or feel so horrible and promise never to do it again. But I did do it again and again. And the reality was that I had not displayed my bad behavior to anyone other than my husband and children. Therefore, there was no one else who could really put me in my place about my dirty little secret.

I have apologized so much that my face should really be blue. No matter how much I apologized, I always reverted back to my old ways because there was always a payoff. Then, one day, the things that I feared the most happened. One particular day, two of my children got into a big disagreement. In an effort to allow my children to have time to work out their differences, I overheard Child A verbally slaughtering Child B. It was so bad that when I came around the corner Child B was in tears and cowering. Child B could not get a word in because Child A was dominating her. This was not the loving behavior that we had taught our children. This was not the interaction of love, care, and teamwork that we so often speak of. This was the behavior of a bully, and bullying was not ever going to be tolerated in our home, or so I thought. I was distraught for my child. The next thing that ensued could have been a huge disaster. However, what could have been ugly, turned into a life changing moment.

As I was getting ready to vehemently reprimand my child, I heard a voice say,

"Take a good look at yourself."

"Take a good look at the consequences of your actions."

"This is what you have taught your children."

"This is what you have displayed before them."

"What you see and hear, is a clear reflection of you."

To say that I was devastated is an understatement. I was overwhelmed with anger, sadness, disappointment, guilt, and shame. The consequences of my actions were staring me right in the face. That was one of many times that the consequences of my behavior far outweighed the payoff.

There is something that I say to my children all of the time. They can quote it in their sleep:

There are penalties and rewards

for the decisions and choices, you make.

You can either reap the reward or pay

the consequences of what you say and do.

The choice is yours!

That statement not only applies to my children, but it is applicable to you and to me. What you need to know is that yelling, sarcasm, belittling, patronizing, and other inappropriate forms of communication and body language is a CHOICE. It is something that you and I use to have power, to control, to manipulate, or to bring another person into submission for our own gain. This is never right. At no time is yelling necessary unless there is an extreme emergency. As you think about that, I want you to ask yourself this question:

What am I getting out of yelling?

_____

_____

_____

_____

_____

_____

_____

What did I think about the kind of person that I am when I yell?

_____

_____

_____

_____

_____

_____

_____

What would other people think of me if they found out about my dirty little secret?

I have always considered myself to be a transparent person. As you can tell from this book, I really have no problem with telling on myself. However, out of all the things my family and friends know about me, they did not know that I was a yeller. I mean, what did I have to yell about in the first place. I am married to a great guy, I am blessed with the most handsome and beautiful children any mom could ask for, I live in a nice home, and I am God fearing.

However, like most people who have addictions and other problems, I covered up my issue really well. You can say that I was a functional yeller. I never acted out in public. And when I did, it was always when the windows were up so no one could hear me. I was afraid of what people would think when they found out that I was a less than perfect wife and mom. I feared that they would finally know that the "happy homemaker" was a miserable mess. I was embarrassed and ashamed. I was frightened that they would discover the truth that lurked behind the smiling face on our family pictures.

It was not until I wrote a blog post and later confessed on social media that they knew of my issue. And even after my confession, most people swept it under the rug. However, I could no long sweep it under the rug. I had to deal with it, or it was going to destroy me along with everything that I held near and dear. I came out of the closet and exposed my truth to everyone, including people I did not know. I was ready to be free. What about you? Are you ready to be free?

If you are ready to be liberated, I want you to ask yourself the same question that I asked myself. In order to be free of people's thoughts and opinions of you, you have to first deal with them, confront them, and conquer them. After you have done that, you have to be willing to lay it all on the line and expose your truth. There is power and freedom in being transparent about your truth.

What would other people think of me if they found out about my dirty little secret and why would it matter?

_____

_____

_____

_____

_____

_____

_____

_____

3

The Power of
Transparency

The Power of Transparency

I believe that there is power in being transparent with your issues. Until things are brought out of the darkness, newness and healing cannot take place. Until you say you have a problem, you cannot be healed and you cannot be helped. I am not telling you what I heard, I am telling you what I know. We are all tricked into thinking that we are the only ones dealing with whatever problem we have. So much so, that we suffer silently inwardly while we are literally screaming outwardly.

One day after a yelling episode, I decided to challenge myself. Because I wanted some accountability, I took to social media and posted that I was going to challenge myself not to yell for 40 days. I had no idea that that post would open a can of screaming worms. Seconds after I wrote that post my friends and other people I knew asked me when I was starting and how could they be part of the challenge. Days after my first post a friend of mine sent me a text message and asked me to create a private group. Days after creating a private group, there were over 50 people who jumped in to take the challenge. By the time the first round was over, there were over 80 people in the group. Just as we were nearing the end of the challenge, the group members were asking what was going to be next. The only thing I knew to do was to restart the challenge. Once the second round started, there were over 150 people in the group. It was beyond amazing. I had no idea that a movement would be started by my exposing my mess. Every morning I would get up and post something to help myself and others. And almost everyday someone would share with the group what was going on in their world.

As we continued with the 40-day challenge, members of the group would tell me about other people who were not on social media who wanted to get involved. They had no desire to get on social media, but they wanted help in conquering their tone of voice. The beauty of it was that it wasn't just moms and wives who were getting involved. Spouses were taking the challenge together. Bosses were taking the challenge to the office. Men and women from all walks of life and backgrounds were taking the challenge and it was working. Mother/child relationships were being saved. Marriages were being restored. Bosses were interacting with their employees better. People were being built up instead of being torn down. Healing of relationships was happening. All this was taking place because God helped me to be bold and brave enough to tell my dirty little secret.

I am sharing this with you because I want you to know that you are not by yourself. You are not the only one dealing with issues of aggressive and negative yelling, sarcasm, body language, and tone of voice. You are not the only one who has temporarily or permanently damaged relationships because of lack of self-control. While I am not proud to say that I have been there and done that, I am proud to say that I have experienced relational healing and restoration of relationships because I choose to respond and react differently. You can experience that, too. Make a commitment. Take a first step and do the Tone of Voice Tone Down.

4

Tone of Voice
Tone Down

Tone of Voice Tone Down

Day 1

Good Morning Friend!

Proverbs 18:21 NKJV

Death and life are in the power of the tongue, And those who love it will eat its fruit.

Proverbs 18:20-21 MSG

Words satisfy the mind as much as fruit does the stomach; good talk is as gratifying as a good harvest. Words kill, words give life; they're either poison or fruit—you choose.

Today's Thought:

Today and everyday I CHOOSE to use my words, my tone of voice, and my body language to speak life to my spouse, my children, my loved ones, my coworkers, and others. Today and every day, I CHOOSE to use my words, my tone of voice, and my body language to speak life into my loved ones, including my spouse, my children, my friends, my coworkers, and others. I will SPEAK LIFE!

Daily Affirmation and Transformation Page

Today is Going to Be a Great Day Because...

_____

_____

_____

Today has been a Great day because...

_____

_____

_____

Today was challenging because...

_____

_____

_____

Tomorrow will be a better day because I will face my challenges by....

_____

_____

_____

Today I will speak life into myself and to the following person by...

_____

_____

_____

I am committed to this transformation because I realize that the death and life of my relationships are in the power of my tongue, my tone of voice, and my body language.

Day 2

Good Morning Friend!

James 1:19-20 NKJV

So then, my beloved brethren, let every man (and woman) be swift to hear, slow to speak, slow to wrath; for the wrath of man (and woman) does not produce the righteousness of God.

Today's Thought:

Today, I make the CHOICE for my body language, my tone of voice, and my words to produce a good crop in my relationship with others, starting with those in my home. Even though things and people may frustrate me, I CHOOSE to be a producer of good and not evil. I strive for today to be a GREAT day! I will SPEAK LIFE!

Daily Affirmation and Transformation Page

Today is Going to Be a Great Day Because...

_____

_____

_____

Today has been a Great day because...

_____

_____

_____

Today was challenging because...

_____

_____

_____

Tomorrow will be a better day because I will face my challenges by....

_____

_____

_____

Today I will speak life into myself and to the following person by...

_____

_____

_____

I am committed to this transformation because I realize that the death and life of my relationships are in the power of my tongue, my tone of voice, and my body language.

Day 3

Good Morning Friend!

Galatians 5:22-23, 25 NKJV

But the fruit of the Spirit is love, joy, peace, longsuffering, kindness, goodness, faithfulness, gentleness, self-control. Against such there is no law. If we live in the Spirit, let us also walk in the Spirit.

Today's Thought:

I CHOOSE to plant good seeds and I CHOOSE to bear good fruit with my words, my tone of voice, and my body language. My relationships with my spouse, my children, my loved ones, my coworkers, and others are at stake. Today WILL be a GOOD Day! I WILL plant good seeds, and I WILL bear good fruit. I will SPEAK LIFE!

Daily Affirmation and Transformation Page

Today is Going to Be a Great Day Because...

_____

_____

_____

Today has been a Great day because...

_____

_____

_____

Today was challenging because...

_____

_____

_____

Tomorrow will be a better day because I will face my challenges by....

_____

_____

_____

Today I will speak life into myself and to the following person by...

_____

_____

_____

I am committed to this transformation because I realize that the death and life of my relationships are in the power of my tongue, my tone of voice, and my body language.

Day 4

Good Morning Friend!

Psalm 141:3 NIV

Set a guard over my mouth, Lord; keep watch over the door of my lips.

Today's Thought:

Today and every day I CHOOSE to watch my mouth. I CHOOSE to watch my words, my tone of voice, and my body language towards my loved ones and others. Today will be a GREAT day as I watch my mouth. I will SPEAK LIFE!

Daily Affirmation and Transformation Page

Today is Going to Be a Great Day Because...

_____

_____

_____

Today has been a Great day because...

_____

_____

_____

Today was challenging because...

_____

_____

_____

Tomorrow will be a better day because I will face my challenges by....

_____

_____

_____

Today I will speak life into myself and to the following person by...

_____

_____

_____

I am committed to this transformation because I realize that the death and life of my relationships are in the power of my tongue, my tone of voice, and my body language.

Day 5

Good Morning Friend!

Lamentations 3:40 NIV

Let us examine our ways and test them, and let us return to the Lord.

Today's Thought

I WILL control and examine what I say and how I say it. I will SPEAK LIFE!

Daily Affirmation and Transformation Page

Today is Going to Be a Great Day Because...

_____
_____
_____

Today has been a Great day because...

_____
_____
_____

Today was challenging because...

_____
_____
_____

Tomorrow will be a better day because I will face my challenges by....

_____
_____
_____

Today I will speak life into myself and to the following person by...

_____
_____
_____

I am committed to this transformation because I realize that the death and life of my relationships are in the power of my tongue, my tone of voice, and my body language.

Day 6

Good Morning Friend!

Matthew 12:33-35 NKJV

"Either make the tree good and its fruit good, or else make the tree bad and its fruit bad; for a tree is known by its fruit. Brood of vipers! How can you, being evil, speak good things? For out of the abundance of the heart the mouth speaks. A good man out of the good treasure of his heart brings forth good things, and an evil man out of the evil treasure brings forth evil things.

Today's Thought:

Out of the abundance of the heart the mouth speaks. I am a good woman. I am a good man. I will put good things in my heart; therefore, good things will come out of my mouth. I will SPEAK LIFE!

Daily Affirmation and Transformation Page

Today is Going to Be a Great Day Because…

_____
_____
_____

Today has been a Great day because…

_____
_____
_____

Today was challenging because…

_____
_____
_____

Tomorrow will be a better day because I will face my challenges by….

_____
_____
_____

Today I will speak life into myself and to the following person by…

_____
_____
_____

I am committed to this transformation because I realize that the death and life of my relationships are in the power of my tongue, my tone of voice, and my body language.

Day 7

Good Morning Friend

Psalms 19:14 NKJV

Let the words of my mouth and the meditation of my heart Be acceptable in Your sight, O Lord, my strength and my Redeemer.

Today's Thought

Are my thoughts in my heart and words out of my mouth acceptable to God? Is the way I said what I said acceptable to God? I will SPEAK LIFE!

Daily Affirmation and Transformation Page

Today is Going to Be a Great Day Because...

_____

_____

_____

Today has been a Great day because...

_____

_____

_____

Today was challenging because...

_____

_____

_____

Tomorrow will be a better day because I will face my challenges by....

_____

_____

_____

Today I will speak life into myself and to the following person by...

_____

_____

_____

I am committed to this transformation because I realize that the death and life of my relationships are in the power of my tongue, my tone of voice, and my body language.

Day 8

Good Morning Friend!

I am excited because today starts week 2 of the 40 Day Tone of Voice Tone Down. I am expecting great things and great progress from all of us. Today is day 8. Did you know that 8 is the number of new beginnings? Thirty-two more days to go. That being said...

Proverbs 15:28 ESV

The heart of the righteous ponders how to answer, but the mouth of the wicked pours out evil things.

Today's Thought:

I WILL think before I speak. I WILL be mindful of my words, my tone of voice, and my body language. Today WILL be a GOOD day! I will SPEAK LIFE!

Daily Affirmation and Transformation Page

Today is Going to Be a Great Day Because…

_____
_____
_____

Today has been a Great day because…

_____
_____
_____

Today was challenging because…

_____
_____
_____

Tomorrow will be a better day because I will face my challenges by….

_____
_____
_____

Today I will speak life into myself and to the following person by…

_____
_____
_____

I am committed to this transformation because I realize that the death and life of my relationships are in the power of my tongue, my tone of voice, and my body language.

Day 9

Good Morning Friend!

Proverbs 25:28 ESV

A man (or woman) without self-control is like a city broken into and left without walls.

Today's Thought:

I WILL have self-control. I WILL NOT carelessly say or do anything. I WILL protect myself, my spouse, my children, my loved ones, my coworkers, and others even from myself. I will SPEAK LIFE!

Keep Striving!

Daily Affirmation and Transformation Page

Today is Going to Be a Great Day Because...

_____

_____

_____

Today has been a Great day because...

_____

_____

_____

Today was challenging because...

_____

_____

_____

Tomorrow will be a better day because I will face my challenges by....

_____

_____

_____

Today I will speak life into myself and to the following person by...

_____

_____

_____

I am committed to this transformation because I realize that the death and life of my relationships are in the power of my tongue, my tone of voice, and my body language.

Day 10

Good Morning! We have entered Day 10 of the 40 Day Tone of Voice Tone Down. I am so proud that you have committed to doing this. Sure, we have had some good days and not so good days. No matter how your days have been, what matters is that you have made a decision in your heart and taken action to do better and be better as it pertains to your mouth. You have purposed in your heart to not communicate through yelling, raising your voice, sarcasm, or other inappropriate forms of communication. In doing this, you have decided to make a positive investment in your household, your children, your marital relationship, your work relationships, and all others. I am so proud of you. Today is day 10, and we have 30 days to go. We can do this. We cannot afford not to do this. We have so much to gain by conquering this area of our lives. We have a lot at stake if we don't. I encourage you not to grow tired. Let the faces of your loved ones, friends, and others remind you why you need to keep moving forward in the 40 Day Tone of Voice Tone Down. Remember, you are not doing this by yourself. We are in this together. I am in it to win it. Are YOU? With that being said....

Good Morning Friend!

Colossians 4:6 MSG

Be gracious in your speech. The goal is to bring out the best in others in a conversation, not put them down, not cut them out.

Today's Thought:

What I say and how I say it has the power to bring out the best or worst in others. I CHOOSE for my words, my tone of voice, and my body language to bring out the best in others. Today will be a great day. I will SPEAK LIFE!

Daily Affirmation and Transformation Page

Today is Going to Be a Great Day Because...

_____

_____

_____

Today has been a Great day because...

_____

_____

_____

Today was challenging because...

_____

_____

_____

Tomorrow will be a better day because I will face my challenges by....

_____

_____

_____

Today I will speak life into myself and to the following person by...

_____

_____

_____

I am committed to this transformation because I realize that the death and life of my relationships are in the power of my tongue, my tone of voice, and my body language.

Day 11

Good Morning Friend! Today is a new day with new mercies!

Proverbs 21:23 MSG

Watch your words and hold your tongue; you'll save yourself a lot of grief.

Today's Thought:

I will not cause damage or bring grief to my spouse, my children, my loved ones, my coworkers, myself or others with my words, my tone, and my body language. I WILL pursue peace EVEN WHEN IT IS DIFFICULT! I will SPEAK LIFE!

Daily Affirmation and Transformation Page

Today is Going to Be a Great Day Because...

_____

_____

_____

Today has been a Great day because...

_____

_____

_____

Today was challenging because...

_____

_____

_____

Tomorrow will be a better day because I will face my challenges by....

_____

_____

_____

Today I will speak life into myself and to the following person by...

_____

_____

_____

I am committed to this transformation because I realize that the death and life of my relationships are in the power of my tongue, my tone of voice, and my body language.

Day 12

Good Morning Friend!

Luke 6:45

The good person out of the good treasure of his heart produces good, and the evil person out of his evil treasure produces evil, for out of the abundance of the heart his (or her) mouth speaks.

Today's Thought:

The good or evil that comes out of my mouth is a reflection of what is in my heart towards others. I will SPEAK LIFE!

Daily Affirmation and Transformation Page

Today is Going to Be a Great Day Because...

_____

_____

_____

Today has been a Great day because...

_____

_____

_____

Today was challenging because...

_____

_____

_____

Tomorrow will be a better day because I will face my challenges by....

_____

_____

_____

Today I will speak life into myself and to the following person by...

_____

_____

_____

I am committed to this transformation because I realize that the death and life of my relationships are in the power of my tongue, my tone of voice, and my body language.

Day 13

Good Morning Friend!

Ephesians 4:29 NLT

Don't use foul or abusive language. Let everything you say be good and helpful, so that your words will be an encouragement to those who hear them.

Today's Thought:

Even when it is difficult, my words, tone, and body language will not be abusive. HOWEVER, I WILL use my words, my tone of voice, and my body language to bless, encourage, and be a gift to my spouse, my children, my loved ones, my coworkers, and others. I will SPEAK LIFE!

Daily Affirmation and Transformation Page

Today is Going to Be a Great Day Because...

_____

_____

_____

Today has been a Great day because...

_____

_____

_____

Today was challenging because...

_____

_____

_____

Tomorrow will be a better day because I will face my challenges by....

_____

_____

_____

Today I will speak life into myself and to the following person by...

_____

_____

_____

I am committed to this transformation because I realize that the death and life of my relationships are in the power of my tongue, my tone of voice, and my body language.

Day 14

Good Morning Friend!

Proverbs 13:3 NLT

Those who control their tongue will have a long life; opening your mouth can ruin everything.

Today's Thought:

I WILL control my tongue, tone, and body language because I don't want to ruin or damage myself or anyone else. I will SPEAK LIFE!

Daily Affirmation and Transformation Page

Today is Going to Be a Great Day Because...

_____

_____

_____

Today has been a Great day because...

_____

_____

_____

Today was challenging because...

_____

_____

_____

Tomorrow will be a better day because I will face my challenges by....

_____

_____

_____

Today I will speak life into myself and to the following person by...

_____

_____

_____

I am committed to this transformation because I realize that the death and life of my relationships are in the power of my tongue, my tone of voice, and my body language.

Day 15

Good Morning Friend!

Proverbs 18:7 MSG

Fools are undone by their big mouths; their souls are crushed by their words.

Today's Thought:

I will not be a fool. I will not allow my words to ruin me or crush the hearts and spirits of my spouse, my children, my loved ones, my coworkers, and others. I will SPEAK LIFE!

Daily Affirmation and Transformation Page

Today is Going to Be a Great Day Because...

_____

_____

_____

Today has been a Great day because...

_____

_____

_____

Today was challenging because...

_____

_____

_____

Tomorrow will be a better day because I will face my challenges by....

_____

_____

_____

Today I will speak life into myself and to the following person by...

_____

_____

_____

I am committed to this transformation because I realize that the death and life of my relationships are in the power of my tongue, my tone of voice, and my body language.

Day 16

Good Morning Friend!

Psalm 34:12-14 NIV

Whoever of you loves life and desires to see many good days, keep your tongue from evil and your lips from telling lies. Turn from evil and do good; seek peace and pursue it.

Today's Thought:

Although I want to live long, I am not promised tomorrow. My friends, family, and loved ones are not promised tomorrow. Therefore, I WILL be careful of what I say and how I say it. I will be peaceful so I won't regret what comes out of my mouth. I will SPEAK LIFE!

Daily Affirmation and Transformation Page

Today is Going to Be a Great Day Because...

_____

_____

_____

Today has been a Great day because...

_____

_____

_____

Today was challenging because...

_____

_____

_____

Tomorrow will be a better day because I will face my challenges by....

_____

_____

_____

Today I will speak life into myself and to the following person by...

_____

_____

_____

I am committed to this transformation because I realize that the death and life of my relationships are in the power of my tongue, my tone of voice, and my body language.

Day 17

Good Morning Friend!

2 Timothy 1:7 AMP

For God did not give us a spirit of timidity (of cowardice, of craven and cringing and fawning fear), but [He has given us a spirit] of power and of love and of calm and well-balanced mind and discipline and self-control.

Today's Thought:

Yesterday is gone. Today is a new day to be victorious. Today, with the help of the Lord, I will be calm and patient. I will be balanced in my thoughts. God has given me the power to not be explosive towards others, but to have discipline and self-control. I will SPEAK LIFE!

Daily Affirmation and Transformation Page

Today is Going to Be a Great Day Because...

_____
_____
_____

Today has been a Great day because...

_____
_____
_____

Today was challenging because...

_____
_____
_____

Tomorrow will be a better day because I will face my challenges by....

_____
_____
_____

Today I will speak life into myself and to the following person by...

_____
_____
_____

I am committed to this transformation because I realize that the death and life of my relationships are in the power of my tongue, my tone of voice, and my body language.

Day 18

Good Morning Friend!

Today, I want to remind you that you are not by yourself. We are in this together. I want to remind you that God is not requiring us to be perfect; He is requiring us to be better for ourselves, our spouses, our children, our friends, our co-workers, and others. With that being said:

Galatians 6:9-10 MSG

So let's not allow ourselves to get fatigued doing good. At the right time we will harvest a good crop if we don't give up, or quit. Right now, therefore, every time we get the chance, let us work for the benefit of all, starting with the people closest to us in the community of faith.

Today's Thought:

I have committed to be a better me, not a perfect me. I have committed to being better for myself and those that I love, care about, live with, and work with. I started this and I am committed to finishing it. Although every day may not be a good day, it is a better day because I am better. I am better because I am more conscientious about what I think, what I say, how I say it. I will stay on this journey to conquer this area in my life. I owe it to myself and my community of faith and all those I love to be the best me that I can be for myself and for them. I want the fruit of my labor to produce a good crop and a good reward. I want my relationships to be blessed, and they will be because God is a keeper of His word. My present and future relationships are at stake. Therefore, I WILL NOT grow weary and I will not quit. With the help of God, I WILL keep pressing forward and I know I WILL WIN! I will SPEAK LIFE!

Daily Affirmation and Transformation Page

Today is Going to Be a Great Day Because...

_____

_____

_____

Today has been a Great day because...

_____

_____

_____

Today was challenging because...

_____

_____

_____

Tomorrow will be a better day because I will face my challenges by....

_____

_____

_____

Today I will speak life into myself and to the following person by...

_____

_____

_____

I am committed to this transformation because I realize that the death and life of my relationships are in the power of my tongue, my tone of voice, and my body language.

Day 19

Good Morning Friend!

Proverbs 16:24 AMP

Pleasant words are as a honeycomb, sweet to the mind and healing to the body.

Today's Thought:

Even if things aren't going my way and when others are being contrary, I CHOOSE to say the right thing and do the right thing. I CHOOSE not to harm anyone with my words or behavior. I make the CHOICE for my words and actions to be gentle and not abrasive. Starting with my household, I make the CHOICE for my words and actions to bring mental, emotional, and physical healing to everyone around me. I will SPEAK LIFE!

Daily Affirmation and Transformation Page

Today is Going to Be a Great Day Because...

_____

_____

_____

Today has been a Great day because...

_____

_____

_____

Today was challenging because...

_____

_____

_____

Tomorrow will be a better day because I will face my challenges by....

_____

_____

_____

Today I will speak life into myself and to the following person by...

_____

_____

_____

I am committed to this transformation because I realize that the death and life of my relationships are in the power of my tongue, my tone of voice, and my body language.

Day 20

Do you know what today is? It is day 20 of our 40 Day journey together. YES, we are at the half way point. I don't know about you but these past 20 days have been life changing for me. I thank God that we are at this place and that I have all of you on my team. You gals and guys are a blessing to me. At some point today, can you please let me know something positive that has happened to you while being on this journey, I would love to read your progress and celebrate you. I especially would like to read about how this journey is impacting the spouses that are doing this together.

Ok, without further ado...

Good Morning Friend!

Philippians 4:13 NKJV

I can do all things through Christ who strengthens me.

Today's Thought:

God is my ultimate HELPER. He gives me strength and empowers me to watch my tone of voice and body language and to have self-control towards others. Because He is on this journey with me, I can do it...I can do anything. I will SPEAK LIFE!

Daily Affirmation and Transformation Page

Today is Going to Be a Great Day Because...

_____

_____

_____

Today has been a Great day because...

_____

_____

_____

Today was challenging because...

_____

_____

_____

Tomorrow will be a better day because I will face my challenges by....

_____

_____

_____

Today I will speak life into myself and to the following person by...

_____

_____

_____

I am committed to this transformation because I realize that the death and life of my relationships are in the power of my tongue, my tone of voice, and my body language.

Day 21

Good Morning Friend!

Proverbs 21:9 AMP

It is better to dwell in a corner of the housetop [on the flat oriental roof, exposed to all kinds of weather] than in a house shared with a nagging, quarrelsome, and faultfinding woman.

Today's Thought:

My home will be a safe haven for my spouse, my children, my friends, my loved ones, and for anyone else who walks through my door. My home will be a place where those who live with me will desire to come home to. I WILL NOT be a man or woman who stirs up strife, who argues, nags, nitpicks, and finds problems with others. I will demonstrate grace and mercy towards others because God shows grace and mercy to me every single day. I will SPEAK LIFE!

Daily Affirmation and Transformation Page

Today is Going to Be a Great Day Because...

_____

_____

_____

Today has been a Great day because...

_____

_____

_____

Today was challenging because...

_____

_____

_____

Tomorrow will be a better day because I will face my challenges by....

_____

_____

_____

Today I will speak life into myself and to the following person by...

_____

_____

_____

I am committed to this transformation because I realize that the death and life of my relationships are in the power of my tongue, my tone of voice, and my body language.

Day 22

Good Morning Friend!

Can you believe that today starts week four of our journey together? I don't know about you but this excites and empowers me. If you don't mind my saying, I am so proud of all of us. You may have had some bumps in the road. You may have had a few disappointments. You may have wanted to quit. But I just want to remind you that quitters never win, and winners never quit. I want you to look at the faces and lives depending on you. Remember that you have a lot at stake if you quit, and you have a lot to gain if you just keep pressing towards the mark. With that being said:

Philippians 3:12-14 MSG

I'm not saying that I have this all together, that I have it made. But I am well on my way, reaching out for Christ, who has so wondrously reached out for me. Friends, don't get me wrong: By no means do I count myself an expert in all of this, but I've got my eye on the goal, where God is beckoning us onward—to Jesus. I'm off and running, and I'm not turning back.

Today's Thought:

I have started this journey and I am going to finish it. I have a goal and with God's help, I will meet my goal. I have come this far, and I can't turn back now. My marriage, my children, my friendships, my work relationships, and possibly other relationships are counting on me to conquer this area of my life. With God's help I WILL WIN! I will SPEAK LIFE!

Daily Affirmation and Transformation Page

Today is Going to Be a Great Day Because...

_____

_____

_____

Today has been a Great day because...

_____

_____

_____

Today was challenging because...

_____

_____

_____

Tomorrow will be a better day because I will face my challenges by....

_____

_____

_____

Today I will speak life into myself and to the following person by...

_____

_____

_____

I am committed to this transformation because I realize that the death and life of my relationships are in the power of my tongue, my tone of voice, and my body language.

Day 23

Good Morning Friend!

Proverbs 15:4 AMP

A gentle tongue [with its healing power] is a tree of life, but willful contrariness in it breaks down the spirit.

Today's Thought:

My words, tone, and body language have the ability to bring healing or destruction to every person that I come in contact with. I realize in times past that my words, tone, and body language have not been used to heal but to hurt. TODAY, starting with those in my house, I make the CHOICE to be a life saver. I CHOOSE to speak life, I CHOOSE to build up and not tear down, and I CHOOSE to mend and not break the hearts and spirits of my spouse, my children, my loved ones, my coworkers, and others. I will SPEAK LIFE!

Daily Affirmation and Transformation Page

Today is Going to Be a Great Day Because...

_____

_____

_____

Today has been a Great day because...

_____

_____

_____

Today was challenging because...

_____

_____

_____

Tomorrow will be a better day because I will face my challenges by....

_____

_____

_____

Today I will speak life into myself and to the following person by...

_____

_____

_____

I am committed to this transformation because I realize that the death and life of my relationships are in the power of my tongue, my tone of voice, and my body language.

Day 24

A bit in the mouth of a horse controls the whole horse. A small rudder on a huge ship in the hands of a skilled captain sets a course in the face of the strongest winds. A word out of your mouth may seem of no account, but it can accomplish nearly anything—or destroy it!Thought: My words, tone of voice, and body language have the ability to greatly build up or destroy my spouse, my children, my loved ones, my coworkers, and anyone who I come in contact with. Even when I am frustrated, I CHOOSE to be a constructive and not a destructive force in my house, at work, or wherever I go.

Good Morning Friend!

James 3:3-5 MSG

A bit in the mouth of a horse controls the whole horse. A small rudder on a huge ship in the hands of a skilled captain sets a course in the face of the strongest winds. A word out of your mouth may seem of no account, but it can accomplish nearly anything—or destroy it!

Today's Thought:

My words, tone of voice, and body language have the ability to greatly build up or to destroy. Even when I am frustrated, I CHOOSE to be a constructive and not a destructive force in my house, at work, or wherever I go. I will SPEAK LIFE!

Daily Affirmation and Transformation Page

Today is Going to Be a Great Day Because...

_____
_____
_____
_____

Today has been a Great day because...

_____
_____
_____
_____

Today was challenging because...

_____
_____
_____
_____

Tomorrow will be a better day because I will face my challenges by....

_____
_____
_____
_____

Today I will speak life into myself and to the following person by...

_____
_____
_____
_____

I am committed to this transformation because I realize that the death and life of my relationships are in the power of my tongue, my tone of voice, and my body language.

Day 25

Good Morning Friend!

A portion of today is directed to those of us who have been blessed to have children or raise someone else's child. Sometimes as parents we think that nobody understands our plight. Being a mom of seven, I want you to know that I understand, and God understands, also. With that being said...

Psalm 127:3-5 MSG

Don't you see that children are God's best gift? the fruit of the womb his generous legacy? Like a warrior's fistful of arrows are the children of a vigorous youth. Oh, how blessed are you parents, with your quivers full of children! Your enemies don't stand a chance against you; you'll sweep them right off your doorstep.

Ephesians 6:4 AMP

Fathers, do not irritate and provoke your children to anger [do not exasperate them to resentment], but rear them [tenderly] in the training and discipline and the counsel and admonition of the Lord.

James 3:5-6 MSG

It only takes a spark, remember, to set off a forest fire. A careless or wrongly placed word out of your mouth can do that. By our speech we can ruin the world, turn harmony to chaos, throw mud on a reputation, send the whole world up in smoke and go up in smoke with it, smoke right from the pit of hell.

Today's Thought:

My children are a gift and blessing from God. God gave my children to me and He gave me to my children. God knows my bent and the bent of my children. There are times that I am overwhelmed. There are times that I feel like I don't know what I am doing. There are times that I am very frustrated. No matter what, I AM CAPABLE of parenting my children. If that were not so, God would not have given us to each other.

I CHOOSE to be a parent who is loving and tender. I CHOOSE to be a parent that will not provoke my children to anger with the things I do or say. I CHOOSE to be a parent that will build up and not tear down my children. I CHOOSE for my words to heal and produce a generation which will heal. I CHOOSE to be a parent that has self-control. I CHOOSE to be a parent that will not break the heart or the spirit of my children. Whether it be one, two, or many, I CHOOSE to be a good steward over the gift that God blessed me with in the form of my children. I will SPEAK LIFE!

Daily Affirmation and Transformation Page

Today is Going to Be a Great Day Because...

_____

_____

_____

Today has been a Great day because...

_____

_____

_____

Today was challenging because...

_____

_____

_____

Tomorrow will be a better day because I will face my challenges by....

_____

_____

_____

Today I will speak life into myself and to the following person by...

_____

_____

_____

I am committed to this transformation because I realize that the death and life of my relationships are in the power of my tongue, my tone of voice, and my body language.

Day 26

Good Morning Friend!

Proverbs 29:11 NASB

A fool always loses his temper, But a wise man holds it back.

Today's Thought:

Some days are more frustrating than others. I recognize that I cannot control everything, BUT I can control how I respond to people and circumstances. I WILL NOT be hasty, quick tempered, and without self-control. I WILL think before I speak and I WILL weigh the consequences for my verbal and non-verbal responses towards others. TODAY IS A GOOD DAY! I will SPEAK LIFE!

Daily Affirmation and Transformation Page

Today is Going to Be a Great Day Because...

_____

_____

_____

Today has been a Great day because...

_____

_____

_____

Today was challenging because...

_____

_____

_____

Tomorrow will be a better day because I will face my challenges by....

_____

_____

_____

Today I will speak life into myself and to the following person by...

_____

_____

_____

I am committed to this transformation because I realize that the death and life of my relationships are in the power of my tongue, my tone of voice, and my body language.

Day 27

Good Morning Friend!

We have just 13 days to go. Are you excited and proud of yourself? I am and I am cheering us all the way to the finish line.

Matthew 12:36-37 MSG

"Let me tell you something: Every one of these careless words is going to come back to haunt you. There will be a time of Reckoning. Words are powerful; take them seriously. Words can be your salvation. Words can also be your damnation."

Matthew 12:36-37 ESV

I tell you, on the day of judgment people will give account for every careless word they speak, for by your words you will be justified, and by your words you will be condemned."

Today's Thought:

I realize that when I stand before God, I will give an account for every word that has come out of my mouth. I will especially have to give an account for my words that have hurt and harmed my spouse, my children and anyone else who have been harmed, torn down, belittled, patronized, pained, and damaged by my words. Today and every day, I CHOOSE for my words to speak life to everyone I come in contact with starting with my family. I will SPEAK LIFE!

Daily Affirmation and Transformation Page

Today is Going to Be a Great Day Because…

_____
_____
_____
_____

Today has been a Great day because…

_____
_____
_____
_____

Today was challenging because…

_____
_____
_____
_____

Tomorrow will be a better day because I will face my challenges by….

_____
_____
_____
_____

Today I will speak life into myself and to the following person by…

_____
_____
_____
_____

I am committed to this transformation because I realize that the death and life of my relationships are in the power of my tongue, my tone of voice, and my body language.

Day 28

Good Morning Friend!

1 Corinthians 6:12 MSG

Just because something is technically legal doesn't mean that it's spiritually appropriate. If I went around doing whatever I thought I could get by with, I'd be a slave to my whims.

Today's Thought:

There are times when I have used my words, tone of voice, and body language to hurt or control others. Especially when I am frustrated, I feel justified in saying and doing what I want. However, just because I can say it or do it, doesn't mean that it is right. I CHOOSE to have self-control, and not say whatever comes to my mind. I WILL NOT allow my mouth and feelings to control or get the best of me. Not only will I consider the time and place of my words and actions, I WILL also consider the consequences. I WILL control my mouth. My mouth WILL NOT control me. I WILL THINK BEFORE I SPEAK! I will SPEAK LIFE!

Daily Affirmation and Transformation Page

Today is Going to Be a Great Day Because...

_____
_____
_____
_____

Today has been a Great day because...

_____
_____
_____
_____

Today was challenging because...

_____
_____
_____
_____

Tomorrow will be a better day because I will face my challenges by....

_____
_____
_____
_____

Today I will speak life into myself and to the following person by...

_____
_____
_____
_____

I am committed to this transformation because I realize that the death and life of my relationships are in the power of my tongue, my tone of voice, and my body language.

Day 29

Good Morning Friend!

Psalm 34:12-14 NIV

Whoever of you loves life and desires to see many good days, keep your tongue from evil and your lips from telling lies. Turn from evil and do good; seek peace and pursue it.

Today's Thought:

Wherever I go, I want to be an example of what it means to be a good and peaceful person. When things don't go my way or when people upset me, I CHOOSE to say the right thing and do the right thing. I want my days on this earth to be good and long. Therefore, I CHOOSE to create an environment of joy and peace so that others will want to be around me. I CHOOSE to pursue peace. Today WILL be a good day! I will SPEAK LIFE!

Daily Affirmation and Transformation Page

Today is Going to Be a Great Day Because...

_____
_____
_____

Today has been a Great day because...

_____
_____
_____

Today was challenging because...

_____
_____
_____

Tomorrow will be a better day because I will face my challenges by....

_____
_____
_____

Today I will speak life into myself and to the following person by...

_____
_____
_____

I am committed to this transformation because I realize that the death and life of my relationships are in the power of my tongue, my tone of voice, and my body language.

Day 30

Good Morning Friend!

Proverbs 15:1-2 NIV

A gentle answer turns away wrath, but a harsh word stirs up anger. The tongue of the wise adorns knowledge, but the mouth of the fool gushes folly.

Today's Thought:

Truthfully, there are things that have the ability to frustrate me and get on my nerves. Some of those I can control and some things I cannot control. No matter who or what comes my way, I can prepare to control how I respond to expected and unexpected situations. When things or people try to stir up my temper or take me to a place where I feel like I am going to lose control and say the wrong thing or respond in a wrong way, I CHOOSE to take control by controlling my tone of voice, my, words, and my body language. I make the CHOICE to be the calm in the storm. I make the CHOICE to not say or do foolish things when foolishness arises. I make the CHOICE to WIN! Today is going to be a GOOD day! I will SPEAK LIFE!

Daily Affirmation and Transformation Page

Today is Going to Be a Great Day Because...

_____
_____
_____
_____

Today has been a Great day because...

_____
_____
_____
_____

Today was challenging because...

_____
_____
_____
_____

Tomorrow will be a better day because I will face my challenges by....

_____
_____
_____
_____

Today I will speak life into myself and to the following person by...

_____
_____
_____
_____

I am committed to this transformation because I realize that the death and life of my relationships are in the power of my tongue, my tone of voice, and my body language.

Day 31

Good Morning Friend!

1 Corinthians 9:24-27 MSG

You've all been to the stadium and seen the athletes' race. Everyone runs; one wins. Run to win. All good athletes train hard. They do it for a gold medal that tarnishes and fades. You're after one that's gold eternally. I don't know about you, but I'm running hard for the finish line. I'm giving it everything I've got. No sloppy living for me! I'm staying alert and in top condition. I'm not going to get caught napping, telling everyone else all about it and then missing out myself.

Today's Thought:

I am determined to win the race/battle of watching my tone of voice, my body language, and my use of sarcasm. I realize that this is not something to take lightly. The life of my relationship with my spouse, my children, my loved ones, my coworkers, and others depends on my winning the race. This race that I am running is not just for 40 days; I am running this race for a lifetime. I want the prize. I want the gold. My prize is for God to be pleased and for me to have happy and healthy relationships with those close to me. I am DETERMINED TO WIN. I will SPEAK LIFE!

Daily Affirmation and Transformation Page

Today is Going to Be a Great Day Because...

_____
_____
_____
_____

Today has been a Great day because...

_____
_____
_____
_____

Today was challenging because...

_____
_____
_____
_____

Tomorrow will be a better day because I will face my challenges by....

_____
_____
_____
_____

Today I will speak life into myself and to the following person by...

_____
_____
_____
_____

I am committed to this transformation because I realize that the death and life of my relationships are in the power of my tongue, my tone of voice, and my body language.

Day 32

Good Morning Friend!

Matthew 15:17-19 NIV

"Don't you see that whatever enters the mouth goes into the stomach and then out of the body? But the things that come out of a person's mouth come from the heart, and these defile them. For out of the heart come evil thoughts—murder, adultery, sexual immorality, theft, false testimony, slander.

Today's Thought:

What is in my heart comes out of my mouth. I don't want to be a man or woman who has no self-control and just says anything. I don't want my words, my tone of voice, or my body language to be to the detriment of anyone. What I say and how I say it is a clear reflection of the type of man or woman I am. Even when things get rough, I CHOOSE to examine my heart before I say anything. I CHOOSE to use my mouth for good because I am a good person. I will SPEAK LIFE!

Daily Affirmation and Transformation Page

Today is Going to Be a Great Day Because...

_____
_____
_____

Today has been a Great day because...

_____
_____
_____

Today was challenging because...

_____
_____
_____

Tomorrow will be a better day because I will face my challenges by....

_____
_____
_____

Today I will speak life into myself and to the following person by...

_____
_____
_____

I am committed to this transformation because I realize that the death and life of my relationships are in the power of my tongue, my tone of voice, and my body language.

Day 33

Good Morning Friend!

Psalm 17:3 NIV

Though you probe my heart, though you examine me at night and test me.

Today's Thought:

There are so many expected and unexpected things that happened throughout the course of my day. It is usually the unexpected things that throw off my day and cause me frustrations. No matter what happens throughout my day, I CHOOSE to have self-control and I CHOOSE to control my responses. At the end of each day I want to have the victory and be able to say that I have not sinned with my words, my tone of voice, and my body language. At the end of the day I want God to examine me and say, "Well done!" I will SPEAK LIFE!

Daily Affirmation and Transformation Page

Today is Going to Be a Great Day Because...

_____

_____

_____

Today has been a Great day because...

_____

_____

_____

Today was challenging because...

_____

_____

_____

Tomorrow will be a better day because I will face my challenges by....

_____

_____

_____

Today I will speak life into myself and to the following person by...

_____

_____

_____

I am committed to this transformation because I realize that the death and life of my relationships are in the power of my tongue, my tone of voice, and my body language.

Day 34

Good Morning Friend!

Ephesians 4:1-3 NIV

As a prisoner for the Lord, then, I urge you to live a life worthy of the calling you have received. Be completely humble and gentle; be patient, bearing with one another in love. Make every effort to keep the unity of the Spirit through the bond of peace.

Today's Thought:

I have been given a great responsibility of being a spouse, a parent, a friend, a loved one, a coworker, and a leader. If God did not think I was worthy of such a great responsibility, He would not have given it to me. I don't take my responsibility lightly. Therefore, instead of losing self-control with my words, my tone of voice, and body language, I CHOOSE to be a person, of peace, gentleness, patience, humility, and love. I will SPEAK LIFE!

Daily Affirmation and Transformation Page

Today is Going to Be a Great Day Because…

_____

_____

_____

Today has been a Great day because…

_____

_____

_____

Today was challenging because…

_____

_____

_____

Tomorrow will be a better day because I will face my challenges by….

_____

_____

_____

Today I will speak life into myself and to the following person by…

_____

_____

_____

I am committed to this transformation because I realize that the death and life of my relationships are in the power of my tongue, my tone of voice, and my body language.

Day 35

Good Morning Friend!

Philippians 4:13 NKJV

I can do all things through Christ who strengthens me.

Today's Thought:

Because the Ultimate Team Player is on my team, I have the ability to have self-control. I CAN control my tone of voice, I CAN control my body language, I CAN control the words that come out of my mouth. I CAN and I WILL have a good day. I will SPEAK LIFE!

Daily Affirmation and Transformation Page

Today is Going to Be a Great Day Because...

_____
_____
_____

Today has been a Great day because...

_____
_____
_____

Today was challenging because...

_____
_____
_____

Tomorrow will be a better day because I will face my challenges by....

_____
_____
_____

Today I will speak life into myself and to the following person by...

_____
_____
_____

I am committed to this transformation because I realize that the death and life of my relationships are in the power of my tongue, my tone of voice, and my body language.

Day 36

My how time flies! Can you believe we have been on this journey together for 36 days? Where has the time gone? Before I get too emotional...

Good Morning Friend!

1 Corinthians 13:4-10 The Message (MSG)

If I give everything I own to the poor and even go to the stake to be burned as a martyr, but I don't love, I've gotten nowhere. So, no matter what I say, what I believe, and what I do, I'm bankrupt without love.

Love never gives up. Love cares more for others than for self. Love doesn't want what it doesn't have. Love doesn't strut, Doesn't have a swelled head, Doesn't force itself on others, Isn't always "me first," Doesn't fly off the handle, Doesn't keep score of the sins of others, Doesn't revel when others grovel, Takes pleasure in the flowering of truth, Puts up with anything, Trusts God always, Always looks for the best, Never looks back, But keeps going to the end.

Love never dies.

Today's Thought:

We all want to be loved. Without love we will all die. Because I need and desire to be loved, I need to BE love and to SHOW love to others, starting with those in my household. I don't want my words, my tone of voice, or my body language to be the death of my relationship with my spouse, my children, or anyone else. No matter how hard or frustrating things get, I CHOOSE to BE LOVE and SHOW LOVE. I will SPEAK LIFE!

Daily Affirmation and Transformation Page

Today is Going to Be a Great Day Because...

_____
_____
_____

Today has been a Great day because...

_____
_____
_____

Today was challenging because...

_____
_____
_____

Tomorrow will be a better day because I will face my challenges by....

_____
_____
_____

Today I will speak life into myself and to the following person by...

_____
_____
_____

I am committed to this transformation because I realize that the death and life of my relationships are in the power of my tongue, my tone of voice, and my body language.

Day 37

Good Morning Friend!

Matthew 7:12 NIV

So in everything, do to others what you would have them do to you, for this sums up the Law and the Prophets.

Today's Thought:

It is selfish to expect someone to do something for me that I am not willing to do for them. It is selfish for me to want love, honor, and respect and not show love, honor, and respect to others. I CHOOSE to treat people the way I want to be treated even when I don't feel like it and when things don't go my way. It is disrespectful for anyone to talk and treat me any kind of way and vice versa. I CHOOSE for my words, body language, and tone of voice to be loving, honorable, and respectful. Sometimes I have been a bad example of treating others the way I want to be treated. But today and every day, I make the CHOICE and give continuous effort to being the example of what love, honor, and respect truly is, starting with those in my home. I CHOOSE to be love. I CHOOSE to be honor. I CHOOSE to be respect. Today is going to be a GREAT day. I will SPEAK LIFE!

Daily Affirmation and Transformation Page

Today is Going to Be a Great Day Because...

_____

_____

_____

Today has been a Great day because...

_____

_____

_____

Today was challenging because...

_____

_____

_____

Tomorrow will be a better day because I will face my challenges by....

_____

_____

_____

Today I will speak life into myself and to the following person by...

_____

_____

_____

I am committed to this transformation because I realize that the death and life of my relationships are in the power of my tongue, my tone of voice, and my body language.

Day 38

Good Morning Friend!

Proverbs 10:31 MSG

A good person's mouth is a clear fountain of wisdom; a foul mouth is a stagnant swamp.

Today's Thought:

I make the CHOICE for my words, my tone of voice, and my body language to exude and pour out love, peace, kindness, gentleness, wisdom, understanding, and all that is good on to my spouse, my children, my loved ones, my coworkers, and others. I CHOOSE for my words, tone of voice, and body language to be a constant stream that gives and speaks life into others, starting with those in my home. I WILL NOT have it be said that my word or actions stagnated and killed my relationships. Even on a bad day, I CHOOSE for my words, my mouth, my tone of voice, and body language to be a force that is a life saver, not a life taker. I CHOOSE for today to be a GREAT day! I will SPEAK LIFE!

Daily Affirmation and Transformation Page

Today is Going to Be a Great Day Because…

_____

_____

_____

Today has been a Great day because…

_____

_____

_____

Today was challenging because…

_____

_____

_____

Tomorrow will be a better day because I will face my challenges by….

_____

_____

_____

Today I will speak life into myself and to the following person by…

_____

_____

_____

I am committed to this transformation because I realize that the death and life of my relationships are in the power of my tongue, my tone of voice, and my body language.

Day 39

Good Morning Friend!

We have one more day to go. I am so proud and excited for us. I have so much to say, but I will save it.

Proverbs 10:11 MSG

The mouth of a good person is a deep, life-giving well, but the mouth of the wicked is a dark cave of abuse.

Today's Thought:

Today and every day I CHOOSE for my words, my tone of voice, and my body language to be tools of good and not evil. I CHOOSE for my mouth and words to be a giver and not a taker of life. I CHOOSE to use my mouth, my tone of voice, my body language, and my words to encourage and empower others. Even on a bad day when things don't go my way, I WILL NOT be a VERBAL ABUSER. I CHOOSE for my mouth, my tone of voice, and my body language to be a well that is overflowing with life. Today is going to be a life giving day. I will SPEAK LIFE!

Daily Affirmation and Transformation Page

Today is Going to Be a Great Day Because…

_____
_____
_____

Today has been a Great day because…

_____
_____
_____

Today was challenging because…

_____
_____
_____

Tomorrow will be a better day because I will face my challenges by….

_____
_____
_____

Today I will speak life into myself and to the following person by…

_____
_____
_____

I am committed to this transformation because I realize that the death and life of my relationships are in the power of my tongue, my tone of voice, and my body language.

Day 40

Good Morning Friend!

I can't believe that 40 days have come so quickly. I don't know about you, but I have enjoyed and have been truly blessed on this journey with all of you. Before I get too sappy, here is todays post. I will express the rest of my thoughts with all of you later today or tomorrow.

1 Peter 3:8-12 MSG

Summing up: Be agreeable, be sympathetic, be loving, be compassionate, be humble. That goes for all of you, no exceptions. No retaliation. No sharp-tongued sarcasm. Instead, bless—that's your job, to bless. You'll be a blessing and also get a blessing. Whoever wants to embrace life and see the day fill up with good, here's what you do: say nothing evil or hurtful; snub evil and cultivate good; run after peace for all your worth. God looks on all this with approval, listening and responding well to what He's asked; But He turns His back on those who do evil things.

Today's Thought:

I CHOOSE to hide today's scripture in my heart and keep it at the forefront of my mind. I CHOOSE to count the cost of my words, my tone of voice, and my body language. I hold dear and value my relationships. I know that there is A LOT at stake in my CHOOSING or NOT CHOOSING to conquer this area of my life. I CHOOSE to be victorious. I WILL be victorious because I can do all things through Christ Who gives me strength. Today will be a good day and tomorrow will be a better day. I CHOOSE to WIN!!! I AM WINNING!!! I WILL CONTINUE TO WIN!!!! I AM A WINNER! I will SPEAK LIFE!

Daily Affirmation and Transformation Page

Today is Going to Be a Great Day Because...

_____
_____
_____

Today has been a Great day because...

_____
_____
_____

Today was challenging because...

_____
_____
_____

Tomorrow will be a better day because I will face my challenges by....

_____
_____
_____

Today I will speak life into myself and to the following person by...

_____
_____
_____

I am committed to this transformation because I realize that the death and life of my relationships are in the power of my tongue, my tone of voice, and my body language.

5

You Did It!!!
What's Next?

You Did It!!! What's Next?

I want to congratulate you on completing the 40 Day Tone of Voice Tone Down. Did you ever think 40 days would go by so fast? Me either! The first time I did this, I couldn't believe how fast the time went by. After I was done, my next question was probably the same question that you have. What's next? The next thing for me was to do the 40 Day Tone of Voice Tone Down all over again. I had made good progress. My family had seen and felt the results of my transformation. Not only had my relationships with my husband and children transformed, but the climate in my house had drastically changed for the better. And because I had changed, the way we all interacted with each other changed also. No longer were my loved ones walking on eggshells, waiting and wondering when I was going to explode. No longer were the children yelling and talking over each other. No longer were my husband and I yelling throughout the house to get someone's attention. We were all holding each other accountable for what we said and how we said it. It was amazing and a miracle to see and hear.

To say that all 40 days were perfect and yell free would not be truthful. Like any person in recovery, I had moments where I slipped and yelled. But the wonderful part about it was that I, along with my family, recognized that I wasn't perfect; but I was better and I was getting better every day. Every day that I didn't yell was a day to celebrate. And in our house, we love to celebrate practically everything. Celebrations and cupcakes go hand in hand in the Avery household, especially when we have nine people living in one house.

Whether you decide to do the 40 Day Tone of Voice Tone Down again or not, it is very important that you celebrate. You should celebrate the fact that you committed 40 days of your life to work on yourself and be a better person. You should celebrate the 40 days you did something that will not only change you, but will also change your relationships. You should celebrate the fact that you not only gave yourself a gift, but you gave your loved ones and others the gift of positive tone of voice and interaction. I don't know how you will celebrate, but whatever you do, CELEBRATE!!! You really deserve it!!! And I hope that you are as proud of yourself as I am for you. If I could see you, I would give you a high five and a big (((HUG))). YOU DID IT!!!

6

Words of Self Affirmation

Words of Self Affirmation:

I am good enough

I am valuable

I am capable

I am smart

I am a good person

I am beautiful

I am handsome

I am amazing

I am wonderful

I am creative

I am lovable

I am worthy

I am growing

I am accepted

I am forgiven

I am striving

I am kind

I am strong

I am empowered

I am an original

I am free

I am inspired

I am special

I am grateful

I am fabulous

I am remarkable

I am significant

I am destined

I am brilliant

I am brave

I am bold

I am gentle

I am a good mom

I am a good wife

I am a good dad

I am a good husband

I am a good spouse

I am a good parent

I am a good sibling

I am a good student

I am a good employer

I am a good employee

I am_____

7

Words of Affirmation for Others

Words of Affirmation for Others:

I respect you

I appreciate you

I value you

I love you

You are caring

You are kind

You are strong

You are worthy

You are one of a kind

You are thoughtful

You are creative

You are important

The world is a better place because you are in it.

You are special

You are forgiven

You are incredible

You are capable

I like when you…

I am impressed by…

You inspire me

You make me smile when…

You add to my life by…

You make me want to be a better me because…

I like_____about you

I like the way you_____

You make me laugh by…

I admire you

You make me happy when…

I am thankful for you because…

You are a good person

You are a good mom

You are a good dad

You are a good wife

You are a good husband

You are a good son

You are a good daughter

You are a good sibling

You are a good student

You are a good boss

You are a good employee

You are_____

Charlotte E. Avery

Biography

Charlotte E. Avery is a portrait of phenomenal womanhood. Her passion for advocating for families was born from her own journey of marriage and motherhood. As providence would have it, her experiences would empower women to be fabulous in every area of their lives. From there, Charlotte has grown to reach not only women, but families from all walks of life.

Charlotte is a wife of 14 years, and a mother of 7 bright and vivacious children. Charlotte navigates the joys and challenges of family, faith, and entrepreneurship with her own unique brand of humor, candor, wisdom, and tenacity.

In true entrepreneur form, Charlotte is the author of *No One Ever Told Me... Witty, Practical, And Spiritual Truths About Motherhood.* She is a speaker and The Family Strategist™. She strategically creates systems that help families function effectively and efficiently with the goal of producing a positive lasting legacy. Charlotte is also the COO and co-owner of Integrity United Technologies, an IT firm and the CEO of Mythikos Mommy, LLC and Being Charlotte Avery. Through her brand, Charlotte advocates for women to love themselves, strengthen their families, live authentically, and do it all in style!

Charlotte is a native of the Washington, D.C metropolitan area. She holds a Bachelor of Science in Therapeutic Recreation from Hampton University and a Master of Science in Sports Medicine from the United States Sports Academy. Charlotte continues to challenge women to be great moms, wives, professionals, and most importantly, to be themselves. Her brand continues to grow through her social media audience and word of mouth.

To learn more about books and programs by Charlotte Avery, log on to her website:

www.beingcharlotteavery.com

Also, become friends on social media at:

 @ Being Charlotte Avery

 @ BeingCharlotteA

 @BeingCharlotteAvery

Join a community of new friends who are on the same mission as you as participants of The Tone of Voice Tone Down Challenge by visiting www.toneofvoicetonedown.com

Made in the USA
Middletown, DE
15 November 2016